Of Holy Disobedience

A. J. MUSTE

A PENDLE HILL

Of Holy Disobedience

A. J. MUSTE

NUMBER 64

JANUARY, 1952

PENDLE HILL

WALLINGFORD

PENNSYLVANIA

THE LAND OF PROPAGANDA IS BUILT
ON UNANIMITY

The quotation which follows is from Ignazio Silone's novel, *Bread and Wine*, which was a moving exposition of life under Fascism in Italy. The conversation between a young woman and an anti-Fascist priest takes place in a small Italian town at the end of the invasion of Ethiopia by Italy. During the night, anti-war and anti-Fascist slogans had been written on walls and steps in the town.

Bianchina told Don Paolo she couldn't understand why there was such a lot of fuss about a few inscriptions on the wall.

Don Paolo was surprised, too. He tried to explain it.

"The Land of Propaganda is built on unanimity," he said. "If one man says, 'No,' the spell is broken and public order is endangered. The rebel voice must be stifled."

"Even if the voice is that of a poor, solitary sick man?"

"Even then."

"Even if it belongs to a peaceful man who thinks in his own way, but does nothing evil apart from that?"

"Even then."

These thoughts served to sadden the girl, but gave the man new heart. He felt ashamed of his previous discouragement.

"In the Land of Propaganda," he said, "a man, any man, any little man who goes on thinking with his own head, imperils public order. Tons of printed paper repeat the government slogans; thousands of loud-speakers, hundreds of thousands of manifestoes and leaflets, legions of orators in the squares and at the crossroads, thousands of priests from the pulpit repeat these slogans ad nauseam, to the point of collective stupefaction. But it is enough for one little man to say 'No!' in his neighbor's ear, or write 'No!' on the wall at night, and public order is endangered."

The girl was terrified, but the man was happy again.

"And if they catch him and kill him?" the girl asked.

"Killing a man who says 'No!' is a risky business," the priest replied, "because even a corpse can go on whispering 'No! No! No!' with a persistence and obstinacy that only certain corpses are capable of. And how can you silence a corpse?"

A BOOK which the French writer, Georges Bernanos, wrote in Brazil—to which he had exiled himself because he would not remain in France under Nazi occupation—has just been published in this country. It is entitled *Tradition of Freedom* and is a hymn to freedom, an impassioned warning against obedience and conformity, especially obedience to the modern State engaged in mechanized, total war.

In the closing pages of this work, Bernanos writes:

I have thought for a long time now that if, some day, the increasing efficiency of the technique of destruction finally causes our species to disappear from the earth, it will not be cruelty that will be responsible for our extinction and still less, of course, the indignation that cruelty awakens and the reprisals and vengeance that it brings upon itself . . . but the docility, the lack of responsibility of the modern man, his base subservient acceptance of every common decree. The horrors which we have seen, the still greater horrors we shall presently see, are not signs that rebels, insubordinate, untameable men, are increasing in number throughout the world, but rather that there is a constant increase, a stupendously rapid increase, in the number of obedient, docile men.

It seems to me that this is a true and timely warning. It might serve as a text for a general appeal to American youth to adopt and practice the great and urgent virtues of Holy Disobedience, non-conformity, resistance toward Conscription, Regimentation and War. For the present I want to use Bernanos' words as an introduction to some

3

observations on the discussion regarding the absolute and relative role of these "virtues" which goes on chiefly among pacifists, members of the Historic Peace Churches and other such groups. I think it will be readily apparent, however, that the principles set forth have a wider bearing and merit consideration by all who are concerned about the maintenance of freedom in our time and the abolition of war.

Most believers in democracy and all pacifists begin, of course, with an area of agreement as to the moral necessity, the validity and the possible social value of No-saying or Holy Disobedience. Pacifists and/or conscientious objectors all draw the line at engaging in military combat and most of us indeed at any kind of service in the armed forces. But immediately thereupon questions arise as to whether we should not emphasize "positive and constructive service" rather than the "negative" of refusal to fight or to register; or questions about the relative importance of "resistance" and "reconciliation," and so on. It is to this discussion that I wish to attempt a contribution. It may be that it will be most useful both to young men of draft age and to other readers if we concentrate largely on the quite concrete problem of whether the former should register, conform to other requirements of the Selective Service Act which apply to conscientious objectors and accept or submit to the alternative service required of them under the law as amended in June, 1951; or whether they shall refuse to register, or if they do register or are "automatically" registered by the authorities, shall refuse to conform at the next stage; and in any event refuse to render any alternative service under conscription. We deal, in other words, with the question whether young men who are eligible for it shall accept the IV-E classification or take the more "absolutist," non-registrant position. (For present purposes, consideration of the I-A-O position, the designation used for

4

draftees who are willing to accept service in the armed forces provided this is non-combatant in character, may be omitted. The IV-E classification is the designation used for persons who are on grounds of religious training and belief opposed to participation in any war. Those who are given this classification are required to render alternative service, outside the armed forces and under civilian auspices, and designed to serve "the health, safety and interest of the United States.")

Two preliminary observations are probably necessary in order to avoid misunderstanding. In the first place, in every social movement there are varied trends or emphases, and methods of working. Those who hold to one approach are likely to be very critical of those who take another. Disagreements among those within the same movement may be more intense or even bitter than with those on the outside. I suppose it can hardly be denied that every movement has in it individuals whose contribution is negative, and that such individuals do not all come from within one wing of the movement. Objective evaluation also leads to the view that the cause is forwarded by various methods and through the agency of diverse individuals and groups. But this does not mean that discussion within the movement of trends and methods of work is not useful and essential. Even if it were true that each of several strategies was *equally* valid and useful, it would still be necessary that each be clearly and vigorously presented and implemented in order that the movement might develop its maximum impact.

Secondly, in what I shall have to say I am not passing moral judgment on individual draftees. But from the fact that a pacifist minister should not pass moral condemnation on the young man in his congregation who in obedience to his conscience enlists or submits to conscription, we do not

5

deduce that this minister should abandon his pacifism or cease to witness to it. Similarly, the fact that in the pacifist movement we support various types of COs in following the lead of conscience does not rule out discussion as to the validity and usefulness of various strategies. It is one thing for a young and immature draftee to follow a course which amounts to "making the best of a bad business" and for others to give him sympathetic understanding and help. It is a very different thing for pacifist organizations or churches to advocate such a course or to rationalize it into something other than it really is.

As some of the readers of this statement are likely to be aware, the writer has advocated the non-registrant position. The majority in the pacifist movement probably believe that it is preferable for COs to accept or submit to the alternative civilian service which was required under the World War II Selective Service Act and is now again required under "peacetime conscription."

The varied considerations and arguments which currently enter into the discussion of this choice confronting the youth of draft age tend, as I see it, to fall into three categories, though there is a good deal of overlapping. One set of considerations may be said to center largely around the idea of Christian or human "vocation"; a second set has to do with the problem of "the immature 18-year-old"; the third with the relation of the pacifist and citizens generally to military conscription and the modern Power-State.

The argument for accepting alternative service, under the first category, has been stated somewhat as follows:

God calls us to love and serve our fellowmen. This is for Christians and other pacifists a matter of vocation. If, then, the government in war time, or under peace time conscription, requires some service of mercy or construction from us, which is not obviously and directly a part of war-making, we will raise no objection to undertaking such work. We may even seek, and shall certainly be grateful for the opportunity to demonstrate our desire to be good citizens and helpful members of society, and to show a reconciling spirit.

This question of the meaning and implications of Christian or human vocation in the context of military conscription clearly needs careful analysis.

Conscription and Vocation

The question of his vocation does not or should not arise suddenly for the Christian or any morally sensitive and responsible individual when Congress enacts a conscription law. The committed Christian has presumably been engaged in an occupation and a way of living which he believes to be in accord with the will of God. This need not be some unusual or spectacular occupation. A Christian farmer, factory worker, miner, teacher, raising a family and giving an example of unselfishness to his neighbors; his wife maintaining an unobtrusively wholesome Christian home; the children walking in the footsteps of such parents —all these may be following a true Christian vocation.

Then war or peace time conscription comes along. If these people are pacifists, they hold that direct participation in war or in combat training is inconsistent with a Christian profession and calling. They must, therefore, refuse such participation. At this point the government tells those of them who come under the draft that they must nevertheless render some civilian service within or under the conscription system. In most cases this will be something different from what they have been doing and will involve temporary removal from the home community.

It has for some time troubled me that a good many pacifists of draft age seem ready to acquiesce in this situation and that, furthermore, many who are not directly affected by the draft seem to feel that at such a time they must immediately find something else to do than that which they have been doing—something that is often referred to as "meaningful" or "sacrificial." Was what they were doing then so definitely not meaningful or sacrificial? Unfortunately, this is very likely the case in many instances. But it does not follow, as is seemingly often assumed, that this justifies going into some entirely new work, a "project," as we say, and perhaps preferably some relief work which has some connection with the war effort, something which society will regard as the "equivalent" of support of the war effort. Certainly the fact that a young man of draft age has not been following a meaningful or Christian vocation does not automatically or by itself constitute a warrant for submitting to conscription for so-called civilian service. It may well be that God calls him at this juncture to put meaning into the life he has been living and into the work he was supposed to be doing.

It is certainly incumbent on us to search our hearts as to whether this rush to get into other jobs and to go to distant places may be motivated by fear of men and of the authorities, by a desire to be thought well of, by a dread of the social displeasure or actual legal punishment which might fall upon us if we were to continue quietly at the work which we had been doing, living in the home town when war fever, if not outright hysteria, seizes the people. "If I were still pleasing men," said St. Paul, "I should not be the slave of Christ."

The Normal as Meaningful

I am convinced that our thinking in these matters is often distorted. What God calls men and women to, fundamentally, is to "be fruitful and multiply and replenish the earth and subdue it and have dominion" over the animal creation—to sow the grain, weave the cloth, build homes and temples to the Eternal. That is what most people should be doing most of the time. In fact, unless they did, even the armies would all soon have to stop in their tracks! War comes along and breaks into this normal life of human beings. That it does this is one of the gravest indictments of war. To resist this breaking up of orderly family and community life—not to yield to the subtle and insistent pressure to do something different under the tacit assumption that the normal cannot be meaningful—is one of the great services the people who believe in non-violence and reconciliation may render. "In returning and rest shall ye be saved, in quietness and in confidence shall be your strength."

To look at the matter from another angle, it is sometimes said that it is important that pacifists should make it clear that they can face hardship and danger and are ready to suffer, if need be, on behalf of their convictions. Granted that this is true, it by no means automatically follows that draft-age youths should submit to conscription or that other pacifists should on the advent of war or conscription leave what they are doing for other work. It may well be that the most challenging opportunity to display courage, hardihood and readiness to suffer will be found precisely in the community in which one has been living and in trying to do the ordinary things about which we have been speaking. There is reason to think that some Congressmen may have been influenced in supporting the "deferment," or virtual exemption, for COs under the original 1948 United States Selective Service Act because they were convinced that few who claim to be COs would have the nerve to stand up against the pressure to which one would be subjected as he tried to go his normal way in his home town or college, when others were being drafted and forced to leave home or college. Obviously, only a pacifist who was leading, not a self-indulgent but a disciplined life, who was ready to face danger and suffering and who deeply loved his fellows, could follow such a course. It is possible that some leave the home or college environment not because they wish to face hardship but because they yield to the temptation to try to avoid it.

Let us, after these preliminary observations, try to determine how—from the standpoint of the concept of Christian vocation—the pacifist may judge the action of a government which requires so-called alternative conscript service of him or of his children or fellow-pacifists. There are, so far as I can see, only three possible verdicts. One possibility is to say that the government is demanding that these conscripts shall at least temporarily *abandon* their Christian or true vocation for work to which they clearly are *not* "called." A second possibility is to say that the government is competent in these special circumstances to determine, and has correctly determined, that the alternative service to which it assigns COs constitutes their Christian vocation for the time being. The third possibility is to reason that when the government thus forces a Christian into another occupation, it is performing an unwarranted and sinful act but that the Christian's duty in such a situation is to practice non-resistance. It, therefore, becomes his vocation to undertake the work which is imposed upon him, not because it is in itself somehow good but because non-resistance to evil constitutes Christian behavior.

The first case is easily disposed of. If the individual is convinced that he is being forced out of his Christian or human vocation into something which, therefore, requires him to disobey God or conscience, he has no alternative but to refuse to comply with the State's demand, perhaps resist it non-violently, and take the consequences. He will still probably be forced out of his accustomed place and work but his non-conformity or non-cooperation with the State's demand at this point becomes his true vocation.

The second possible attitude listed a moment ago is to hold that, in the context of conscription and provided it does not require service in the armed forces, the State may determine what one's Christian vocation is. Some of the Mennonite statements and those of some other pacifists seem to me to fall under this head. The position seems to me a very precarious one and I question whether Mennonites, for example, can maintain it as consistent with their own theology and Christian ethics.

The Role of Jehovah's Witnesses

In the first place, it is essential in the Christian concept of vocation that the "call" is from the Spirit speaking in the heart of the believer. And the believer must always remain in a position where he can be free to respond to the prompting of the Spirit. But how can this be under a conscription regime? The position of Jehovah's Witnesses that they cannot submit to conscription because they must always be free to "witness" to the faith, is in this respect surely a strong and impressive one. It has a bearing also, incidentally, on what we said some paragraphs earlier under general observations about Christian vocation. It seems to me that Christian pacifists need to give much more thought than they have done to the question whether in this particular respect the Witnesses, so far from being eccentric, are not taking the clear and consistent, centrally Christian, stand. The fact that the Witnesses can hardly be classified as pacifists in the usual sense of the term does not affect the relevance of this question for pacifists and indeed for Christians generally.

Furthermore in Mennonite thought, government, the State, though it is "an ordinance of God" to curb sin, is itself by definition also sinful, not Christian, not a part of "the order of redemption." Where, then, does the State get the competence, or the mandate to determine, of all things, the *Christian* vocation of a *believer?* And particularly the war-making arm or department of the State? If the war department or its adjunct, Selective Service, is qualified to determine Christian vocation as part of its conduct of, or preparation for, a war, then why should not the labor department in peace time tell Christians where to work?

There remains a third possible position, namely, that the State is undoubtedly doing an evil thing in taking the individual out of the work to which he feels God has called him but that the principle of non-resistance to evil then comes into operation and submission to this evil becomes the vocation of the persecuted Christian. Given certain premises, there is logic in this position, but it is nevertheless open to serious question. In the first place, non-resistance to an evil should not mean cooperation with it. "Depart from evil and do good," is the law. Pacifists in general, and Christian pacifists in particular, have to ask whether in conforming with any of the provisions of a draft law and especially in rendering conscript service regarded as of "national importance" by a war-making state, they are not helping conscription to run smoothly, helping thus to force conscription on millions of youth and thus in turn promoting war, since conscription is an integral part of an armaments race. The phenomenon of increased tension between nations when they lengthen the compulsory service period for youth is a familiar one. This, of course, raises the whole question of our evaluation of the meaning and role of military conscription, to which we shall return later.

In the meantime, one or two other comments need to be made on the phase of our problem under discussion. If what is really happening is that the war-making state is inflicting an evil on people, forcing them away from their vocation, subjecting them to a measure of persecution, then it seems we ought to keep this clearly in our own minds and ought not to let the government or public assume that we think otherwise. The expressions of "gratitude" which we have sometimes heard addressed to government for "permitting" pacifists to render alternative service seem inappropriate. We cannot have it both ways: accuse the State of the grave sin of invading the realm of Christian vocation and at the same time thank it for doing us a "favor" by making the invasion less than total. The State is not doing God or Christian people a favor in recognizing conscience, though that is what most United States Congressmen think they are doing in making some provision for COs. The pacifist who in any way encourages this notion is in danger of helping to give currency to the idea that conscience is a private whim which legislators may see fit to indulge for prudential reasons, as long as those who are afflicted with this peculiarity are very few in numbers. If non-resistant pacifists get off the high ground of patiently bowing the neck to Caesar's yoke, letting Caesar inflict the scourge of civilian conscript service upon them, they are immediately on the low ground of bargaining for indulgence for a small and, in that view, not too principled or brave a minority. Standing on that lower ground they have very little bargaining *power* and the results will reflect that fact—and pretty much did during World War II. On the other hand, both in Great Britain and in the United States the sufferings which the COs endured in World War I when there was virtually no legal or social recognition of them, were, according to all competent observers, largely responsible for the fact that fairly liberal provisions for COs were made in World War II. The Army did not want to "be bothered with these fellows again."

Two Miles or None

This does not, of course, mean that if the imposition of alternative service is accepted, it should be rendered grudgingly or that feelings of hostility toward government officials with whom one may deal are appropriate. Quite the contrary. If we decide to go with Caesar one mile, the Gospel enjoins us to go two! We have the choice of not going along at all or going two miles, but not a skimpy one mile.

I think it is now generally admitted that there was not a great deal of this glad, spontaneous "second miling" on the part of the conscript COs in World War II, though there was considerable talk about it among older folks. Civilian Public Service in large measure simply did not operate on the high spiritual plane that was originally hoped and is still sometimes implied or stated, but was for many making the best of a bad business, perhaps for lack of clear leading or the courage to follow another course.

It will be recalled that there were a considerable number of Civilian Public Service men who declared flatly that it was inconsistent, and indeed hypocritical, to talk of spontaneous service under conscription. "We are here," they said, "not because our desire to serve brought us here. We are here because the government as part of its war program passed a conscription law and under that law took us by the scruff of the neck and is forcing us to do this job. We have no choice but this or the army or jail. That fact is bound to color this whole experience, except perhaps for those who can shut their eyes to reality. Any one who denies this is a hypocrite."

It seems to me these COs placed the finger on an essential point. Compulsion does enter into "service" under a conscription law. It affects the whole picture. Therefore, the evaluation to be made of the IV-E position and of alternative service under it is not disposed of by asserting that "service is at least as real a part of Christian or pacifist life as witness or resistance." That statement is perfectly correct. Service of men, fellowship with them, on the one hand, and non-cooperation with evil, witness against injustice, non-violent resistance, on the other hand, are both essential in the pacifist way of life. There is some of each in every pacifist life. The most "reconciling" one refuses to use a gun or even, probably, to put on a uniform. Some of the most extreme "resisters" in prison were known for the thoughtful and gentle service they rendered to criminal fellow-inmates. A very discerning English pacifist observed: "For some their witness is their service, for others their service is their witness," or resistance. Each type needs to be on guard against the temptations peculiar to it, including the temptation to question the motives or underestimate the contribution of pacifists of the other type.

But the service which is the essence of pacifism is free, spontaneous, joyous, sacrificial, unbought. To magnify or glorify this is by no means automatically to magnify or glorify the IV-E position *under the draft.* Here, as we have pointed out, an element enters which is contradictory to pacifism, freedom and spontaneity—*the element of compulsion in a context of war and war preparation.*

It seems to me that it is important for pacifists to bear this in mind as we make plans to deal with the problem of alternative service under the amended 1948 Selective Service Act. No matter how "liberal" or "considerate" the conditions for administering alternative service may be in the estimation of government officials or the pacifist agencies, if alternative service is accepted or acquiesced in at all, it will inevitably pose grave problems from the standpoint of Christian vocation and it will not, I think, be possible to escape the contamination or corruption which "conscription" infuses into "service." At the moment it seems possible that Selective Service regulations will permit some individuals to remain at their accustomed occupations. We put aside for the time being certain questions to which we shall return as to what the act of registration itself implies in the context of conscription for atomic and biological war. Here we emphasize that once a man has appealed to the State to permit him to remain in his job and has been granted such permission, it is not exactly the same job as it was before. Others will not be given the same permission, and he should not evade the question whether he can acquiesce in and to a degree benefit from such discrimination. He will have to consider whether the consideration in his case arises from the fact that officials regard his work as in some way a contribution to the war effort, or from a desire to placate and silence an influential person. If he should conclude that he ought to change jobs, he would have to consult the authorities again, and what then?

In conferences with Selective Service officials efforts are being made to avoid some of the features of the war-time Civilian Public Service set-up which deeply troubled a good many Friends—such as the close supervision by military men allegedly functioning as civilians and the undesirable and frustrating character of much of the work to which IV-E men were assigned. Even if substantial concessions are obtained, it will be well for us to be on guard against idealizing the situation. It is hoped that a good many young men will be in effect furloughed to projects at home and abroad which will not be exclusively for COs of draft age and which will have real social value. It will not be the same as if these men had undertaken these jobs out of a sense of vocation and mission, apart from the context of conscription. We know that for the most part they did not volunteer until conscription came along. The same questions which the man who is permitted to remain in his own job faces, will confront these young men on projects. In addition, their term of service and rates of pay will be set by the government.

To sum up this first part of our analysis, it is my conclusion that the one consistent attitude toward conscript alternative service from the standpoint of Christian vocation—if one accepts such work at all—is that which regards submission or non-resistance to the evil which the State imposes upon him when it interferes with his normal occupation, as the vocation or duty of the Christian man. Any other attitude seems to me to involve a considerable measure of rationalization. The Mennonites came nearest to adopting this non-resistant position and the fact that the experience of Mennonite youths in Civilian Public Service was less frustrating and brought better results than was the case with others, save in exceptional instances, seems to me to bear out my analysis. As we have pointed out, those who non-resistantly take up their cross of conscription should bear it joyously and be ready to carry it the second mile.

The Immature Eighteen-Year-Old

We turn next to a brief consideration of the arguments for the IV-E as against the non-registrant position which center around the problem of "the immature 18-year-old youth." A number of 18-year-olds, it is pointed out, have a strong aversion to war and a leaning toward pacifism. They are, however, emotionally immature. If they have no choice but the army or jail all but a few will choose the army and are likely to be lost to the pacifist cause. They could be held and possibly even developed into a radical pacifist position, if they had a third choice, namely, civilian service. On the other hand, the youth who in the absence of such a third possibility, chooses prison rather than the army may suffer grave psychological injury.

I am sure no one will be disposed to be callous or "tough" in his attitude toward any youth faced with a problem such as we are discussing. Any one in the position of a counselor to an individual will want to avoid "psychological pressuring" to induce him to take this or that course, and will strive to help the young man to make his own decision, in accord with his own inner need and conviction, rather than to impose a decision upon him. But I conceive that it would be my duty as a Christian minister to have this same attitude in talking and praying with a young man who was going into the Army. I would have no right, nor do I think it would do any good, to "pressure" him against his conviction and inner need, to refuse service. But this would certainly not mean that I give up my own pacifist convictions, or refrain from doing all I can in general to spread them or from making this particular young man aware of my own thoughts and feelings. This in spite of the fact that if young men who had planned to submit to the draft are consequently won to the pacifist position, this may entail considerable suffering on their part, anguish for parents who disagree with them, and so on. It is fairly certain, incidentally, that in many typical Southern communities—and by no means exclusively in the South—a youth who chose the I-A-O (medical corps) position, not to mention IV-E, would have as tough a time as a non-registrant in many metropolitan centers. We cannot, then, escape the conclusion that as we have a responsibility to decide for the pacifist or non-pacifist position and to bear witness for pacifism, if that is the stand we take, so as pacifists we have a responsibility to decide whether complete non-cooperation with military conscription is the more consistent, committed and effective stand or not, and if we decide for the former, then to do what we can to make our stand and the reasons for it known.

I have the impression that even a great many, perhaps the majority, of pacifist ministers will work harder to keep a young pacifist parishioner from taking the "absolutist" position and going to jail rather than into civilian service, than they would work to get the run of the mill young parishioners to think seriously about not going into the army. They seem somehow to feel that a more awful thing is happening to the young CO who goes to jail than to the 18-year-old who goes into the army. It is my impression that this same feeling is an unconscious factor in the thinking of many lay pacifists when they react strongly against the idea of COs going to prison. This puzzles me greatly. Why should they have this reaction?

Army or Jail ?

To my mind—even apart from the sufficiently appalling factor of being systematically trained for wholesale killing and subjected to the risk of being killed in brutal war—there are few if any more evil and perilous situations to put young men into than the armed forces. I should feel much deeper grief over having possibly had some part in getting some youth to go into the armed forces than over having some responsibility for bringing a young man to go to prison for conscience's sake. Are the qualms people feel about youthful COs going to prison in certain instances perhaps due to the fact that taking the non-registrant position is something very unusual and regarded with social disapproval, whereas becoming a soldier is extremely common and meets with the highest social approval? It may be, therefore, that there are some ministers and other older people who should examine themselves as to whether their feelings in the matter under discussion are due to the fact that they themselves might find life in the community or in the church very uncomfortable if they were suspected of having influenced a youth to take a radical anti-draft stand, whereas all men will speak well of them—or at least not too ill—if they have helped, or at least not hindered, young Christians in adjusting themselves to the idea of going into the army. Is it just possible that we older people are sometimes concerned with sparing ourselves when we think we are solely concerned about sparing teen-agers?

To return to the 18-year-old. There are young men who on physical and psychological grounds are exempted from army service. There may well be COs who should on similar grounds be exempted from any kind of service. If such a physically or mentally ill CO is refused exemption, he should perhaps be discouraged from undergoing the risks of prison experience if there is an alternative for him. This still leaves us with the problem of the majority of pacifist and non-pacifist youth who are not ill.

When we find ourselves concerned about what the teen-age religious CO who goes to prison must undergo and inclined to think that there is here an absolutely conclusive case for providing alternative service and urging most such COs to avail themselves of it, we might first take a look at two other categories of youth who are subject to the draft. One of them consists of those actually drafted into the armed services; the other of the so-called non-religious COs.

The great mass of teen-agers are going to be put through rigorous military training with all the hardships, the toughening and the temptations which this entails. They have to be ready to undergo actual battle experience. Many of them will actually experience modern war at the front. Is what the CO undergoes in prison vastly more terrible than this? Is it as terrible? It may be said that the soldier has social approbation whereas the pacifist, especially the "absolutist" meets social disapprobation and even ostracism. This is indeed a sore trial and many cannot endure it. Frankly, I am still left with more grief and pity in my heart for the teen-age soldier than for the teen-age "absolutist" CO. I am still left with a question whether we have a right to take any time and energy away from the struggle to lift the curse of conscription from the mass of youth and put it into an effort o secure alternative conscript service for COs.

There are, as we know, teen-age "absolutists" who feel the same way and who have demonstrated that they can endure whatever they may be called upon to endure. Nor is their lot without its compensations. They, also, "have their reward."

The So-Called Non-Religious CO

Religious COs who accept the IV-E classification and older pacifists who advocate this course have also to consider the non-religious CO. Under United States Law it is the so-called religious CO who is eligible for this classification; the so-called non-religious CO, though he may by unanimous consent be equally sincere, is not. The latter has no choice except the army or jail. The fact that he is only 18 years old does not alter that. Nothing in this entire field of pacifist policy and behavior is, frankly, harder for me to understand than how religious COs and many of the leaders of the peace churches and of the Fellowship of Reconciliation, can acquiesce in this situation and accept what is regarded as an advantage, a preferred position, under it. The white CO who accepted conscript alternative service when the Negro CO was automatically forced to choose the army or prison would be in an invidious position. So would the Gentile when his Jewish comrade was thus discriminated against. But in my mind the case is far more deplorable when it is the religious and the supposedly nonreligious man who are involved. The white man or the Gentile might actually believe in discrimination or not regard it too seriously when the discrimination is in his favor. But for the religious man it should surely be a central and indispensable part of his faith that discrimination, most of all where two men acting in obedience to conscience are involved, is unthinkable and that if there is discrimination, he cannot be the beneficiary of it.

At any rate, the argument that there must be alternative service because *immature* 18-year-olds must by no means be subjected to prison experience seems to me to become completely impotent in the mouths of those religious pacifists who acquiesce in the arrangement under discussion and enable it to work—unless indeed they mean to contend that the average religious CO has less stamina than the non-religious CO and that, therefore, the former should be given gentler treatment.

Advocacy of alternative service for the teen-age CO is based on considerations relating to the future of the pacifist movement, as well as on the effect on the COs themselves. It is argued that if the only choice young pacifists have is the army or jail, there will be very few pacifists. This argument was not, however, first advanced when the draft age was lowered. It was often heard during World War II when most COs were older and more seasoned. It has always impressed me as a dubious argument and I wonder where it leads us. What, for example, is the relationship of this argument to the one which is also advanced—sometimes by the same person—that the IV-E position is very meaningful and perhaps to be preferred to the more "absolutist" one, because it is the IV-E man who gives a glorious demonstration of the spirit of selfless service which is the essence of pacifism at its best? These two concepts cannot very well be harnessed together as a team. We can hardly contend in one and the same breath that we want alternative service because most young pacifists are not ready to follow a stronger and more sacrificial course *and* that we want it because it is the strongest and most meaningful course pacifists can follow. It seems to me we have to decide whether our problem is to find shelter for COs or whether it is to find freedom and the opportunity for self-expression and service, even though the price be high.

To consider the matter for a moment from the tactical viewpoint, it seems quite certain that the number of 18-year-olds who take either the IV-E or the non-registrant position (perhaps even the I-A-O position might be included) will at least at the outset be small. The draft now gets the young man at the very age when it is most difficult for him to stand out in any way from the mass of his fellows. Even if he is intellectually pretty well convinced of the pacifist position, he is not emotionally mature enough to take it. It is a fair guess that the accessions to the pacifist movement, if military service and/or training becomes universal, will in the future come mainly from young people who have gone through the experience of life in the armed forces. In other words, the additional number of pacifists recruited because alternative service is provided may turn out to be very small. If so, the numerical advantage from the adoption of a less uncompromising pacifism is illusory.

There is one other factor which may be mentioned in this context, that we live in an age when the role of minorities is an increasingly difficult one. The pressures and the actual persecution to which they are subjected are severe. The trend is still partially obscured in the United States but if we pause to reflect that not a single bomb has as yet fallen on this country, we shall realize that this country is not an exception to the trend toward greater conformity and regimentation. As the New York *Times* editorialized some time ago in commenting on some features of the McCarran Act, if we are already resorting to such repressive measures, what will we do when a real crisis comes? In other words, while we spend a good deal of time arguing that COs should have some choice other than the army or jail, we are probably moving into a time when that will essentially be the only choice that members of minorities, including pacifists, have. It would seem then that our thought and energy should be devoted to two issues: whether and how this trend toward totalitarianism can be halted and how we may prepare and discipline ourselves to meet the tests which our fellow-pacifists in some other lands have already had to meet?

The Nature of Conscription

This, however, leads to the third and last of the issues we are trying to explore: the true nature of conscription, of modern war, and of the conscripting, war-making State—and the attitude which pacifists consequently should take toward them.

Participation in alternative service is quite often defended on the ground that our opposition is to war rather than conscription; except in the matter of war we are as ready to serve the nation as anybody; therefore, as long as we are not drafted for combat or forced against our will into the armed services, we are ready to render whatever service of a civilian character may be imposed upon us.

Is this a sound position? Let me emphasize that it is conscription for war under the conditions of the second half of the twentieth century that we are talking about. The question as to whether sometime and under some circumstances we might accept conscription for some conceivable purpose not related to war, is not here at stake. It is academic and irrelevant. The question with which we are dealing is that of conscripting youth in and for modern war.

As pacifists we are opposed to all war. Even if recruitment were entirely on a voluntary basis, we would be opposed. It seems to me we might infer from this that we should be *a fortiori* opposed to military conscription, for here in addition to the factor of war itself, the element of coercion by government enters in, coercion which places young boys in a military regime where they are deprived of freedom of choice in virtually all essential matters. They may not have the slightest interest in the war, yet they are made to kill by order. This is surely a fundamental violation of the human spirit which must cause the pacifist to shudder.

The reply is sometimes made that pacifists are *not* being conscripted for military purposes and therefore—presumably—*they* are not faced with the issue of the nature of military conscription. I shall later contend that it is not really possible to separate conscription and war, as I think this argument does. Here I wish to suggest that even if the question is the conscription of non-pacifist youth, it is a fundamental mistake for pacifists ever to relent in their opposition to this evil, ever to devote their energies primarily to securing provisions for COs in a draft law or to lapse into a feeling that conscription has somehow become more palatable if such provisions are made by the State. It is not our own children if we are pacifist parents, our fellow-pacifist Christians if we are churchmen, about whom we should be most deeply concerned. In the first place, that is a narrow and perhaps self-centered attitude. In the second place, pacifist youths have some inner resources for meeting the issue under discussion. The terrible thing which we should never lose sight of, to which we should never reconcile our spirits, is that the great mass of 18-year olds are drafted for war. They are given no choice. Few are at the stage of development where they are capable of making fully rational and responsible choice. Thus the fathers immolate the sons, the older generation immolates the younger, on the altar of Moloch. What God centuries ago forbade Abraham to do even to his own son—"Lay not thy hand upon the lad, neither do thou anything unto him"—this we do by decree to the entire youth of a nation.

We need to ask ourselves whether such conscription is in any real sense a lesser evil. As we have already said, the pacifist is opposed to war and we have all sensed the danger of arguing against conscription *on the ground that* the nation could raise all the troops it needed by voluntary enlistment. Nevertheless, there is a point to an impassioned argument which George Bernanos makes in the book we mentioned at the outset. He states that the man created by western or Christian civilization "disappeared in the day conscription became law . . . the principle is a totalitarian principle if ever there was one—so much so that you could deduce the whole system from it, as you can deduce the whole of geometry from the propositions of Euclid."

To the question as to whether France, the Fatherland. should not be defended if in peril, he has the Fatherland answer: "I very much doubt whether my salvation requires such monstrous behavior" as defense by modern war methods. If men wanted to die on behalf of the Fatherland, moreover, that would be one thing but "making a clean sweep, with one scoop of the hand, of an entire male population" is another matter altogether: "You tell me that, in saving me, they save themselves. Yes, if they can remain free; no, if they allow you to destroy, by this unheard of measure, the national covenant. For as soon as you have, by simple decree, created millions of French soldiers, it will be held as proven that you have sovereign rights over the persons and the goods of every Frenchman, that there are no rights higher than yours and where, then, will your usurpations stop? Won't you presently presume to decide what is just and what is unjust, what is Evil and what is Good?"

It is pretty certainly an oversimplification to suggest, as Bernanos here does, that the entire totalitarian, mechanized "system" under which men today live or into which they are increasingly drawn even in countries where a semblance of freedom and spontaneity remains, can be traced to its source in the military conscription which was instituted by the French Revolution in the eighteenth century. But what cannot, it seems to me, be successfully denied is that today totalitarianism, depersonalization, conscription, war, and the conscripting, war-making power-state are inextricably linked together. They constitute a whole, a "system." It is a disease, a creeping paralysis, which affects all nations, on both sides of the global conflict. Revolution and counter-revolution, "peoples' democracies" and "western democracies," the "peace-loving" nations on both sides in the war, are cast in this mold of conformity, mechanization and violence. This is the Beast which, in the language of the Apocalypse, is seeking to usurp the place of the Lamb.

We know that "war will stop at nothing" and we are

clear that as pacifists we can have nothing to do with it. But I do not think that it is possible to distinguish between war and conscription, to say that the former is and the latter is not an instrument or mark of the Beast.

Disobedience Becomes Imperative

Non-conformity, Holy Disobedience, becomes a virtue and indeed a necessary and indispensable measure of spiritual self-preservation, in a day when the impulse to conform, to acquiesce, to go along, is the instrument which is used to subject men to totalitarian rule and involve them in permanent war. To create the impression at least of outward unanimity, the impression that there is no "real" opposition, is something for which all dictators and military leaders strive assiduously. The more it seems that there is no opposition, the less worthwhile it seems to an ever larger number of people to cherish even the thought of opposition. Surely, in such a situation it is important not to place the pinch of incense before Caesar's image, not to make the gesture of conformity which is involved, let us say, in registering under a military conscription law. When the object is so plainly to create a situation where the individual no longer has a choice except total conformity or else the concentration camp or death; when reliable people tell us seriously that experiments are being conducted with drugs which will paralyze the wills of opponents within a nation or in an enemy country, it is surely neither right nor wise to wait until the "system" has driven us into a corner where we cannot retain a vestige of self-respect unless we say No. It does not seem wise or right to wait until this evil catches up with us, but rather to go out to meet it—to *resist*—before it has gone any further.

As Bernanos reminds us, "things are moving fast, dear

reader, they are moving very fast." He recalls that he "lived at a time when passport formalities seemed to have vanished forever." A man could "travel around the world with nothing in his wallet but his visiting card." He recalls that "twenty years ago, Frenchmen of the middle class refused to have their fingerprints taken; fingerprints were the concern of convicts." But the word "criminal" has "swollen to such prodigious proportions that it now includes every citizen who dislikes the Regime, the System, the Party, or the man who represents them. . . . The moment, perhaps, is not far off when it will seem natural for us to leave the front-door key in the lock at night so that the police may enter at any hour of the day or night, *as it is to open our pocket-books to every official demand.* And when the State decides that it would be a practical measure . . . to put some outward sign on us, why should we hesitate to have ourselves branded on the cheek or on the buttock, with a hot iron, like cattle? The purges of 'wrong-thinkers,' so dear to the totalitarian regimes, would thus become infinitely easier."

To me it seems that submitting to conscription even for civilian service is permitting oneself thus to be branded by the State. It makes the work of the State in preparing for war and in securing the desired impression of unanimity much easier. It seems, therefore, that pacifists should refuse to be thus branded.

In the introductory chapter to Kay Boyle's volume of short stories about occupied Germany, *The Smoking Mountain,* there is an episode which seems to me to emphasize the need of Resistance and of not waiting until it is indeed too late. She tells about a woman, professor of philology in a Hessian university who said of the German experience with Nazism: "It was a gradual process." When the first *Jews Not Wanted* signs went up, 'there was never any protest made about them, and, after a few months, not only we, but even the Jews who lived in that town, walked past without noticing any more that they were there. Does it seem impossible to you that this should have happened to civilized people anywhere?"

The philology professor went on to say that after a while she put up a picture of Hitler in her class-room. After twice refusing to take the oath of allegiance to Hitler, she was persuaded by her students to take it. "They argued that in taking this oath, which so many anti-Nazis had taken before me, *I was committing myself to nothing, and that I could exert more influence as a professor than as an outcast in the town.*"

She concluded by saying that she now had a picture of a Jew, Spinoza, where Hitler's picture used to hang, and added: "Perhaps you will think that I did this ten years too late, and perhaps you are right in thinking this. *Perhaps there was something else we could all of us have done, but we never seemed to find a way to do it, either as individuals or as a group, we never seemed to find a way.*" A decision by the pacifist movement in this country to break completely with conscription, to give up the idea that we can "exert more influence" if we conform in some measure, do not resist to the uttermost—this might awaken our countrymen to a realization of the precipice on the edge of which we stand. It might be the making of our movement.

The Reconciling Resistance

Thus to embrace Holy Disobedience is not to substitute Resistance for Reconciliation. It is to practice both Reconciliation and Resistance. In so far as we help to build up or smooth the way for American militarism and the regimentation which accompanies it, we are certainly not practising reconciliation toward the millions of people in the Communist bloc countries against whom American war preparations, including conscription, are directed. Nor are we practising reconciliation toward the hundreds of millions in Asia and Africa whom we condemn to poverty and drive into the arms of Communism by our addiction to military "defense." Nor are we practising love toward our own fellow-citizens, including also the multitude of youths in the armed services, if, against our deepest insight, we help to fasten the chains of conscription and war upon them.

Our works of mercy, healing and reconstruction will have a deeper and more genuinely reconciling effect when they are not entangled with conscript service for "the health, safety and interest" of the United States or any other war-making State. It is highly doubtful whether Christian mission boards can permit any of their projects in the Orient to be manned by men supposed to be working for "the health, safety and interest" of the United States. The Gospel of reconciliation will be preached with a new freedom and power when the preachers have broken decisively with American militarism. It can surely not be preached at all in Communist lands by those who have not made that break. It will be when we have gotten off the back of what someone has called the wild elephant of militarism and conscription on to the solid ground of freedom, and only then, that we shall be able to live and work constructively. Like Abraham we shall have to depart from the City-which-is in order that we may help to build the City-which-is-to-be, whose true builder and maker is God.

It is, of course, possible, perhaps even likely, that if we set ourselves apart as those who will have no dealings whatever with conscription, will not place the pinch of incense before Caesar's image, our fellow-citizens will stone us, as

31

Stephen was stoned when he reminded his people that it was they who had "received the law as it was ordained by angels, and kept it not." So may we be stoned for reminding our people of a tradition of freedom and peace which was also, in a real sense, "ordained by angels" and which we no longer keep. But, it will thus become possible for them, as for Paul, even amidst the search for new victims to persecute, suddenly to see again the face of Christ and the vision of a new Jerusalem.

Some one may at this point reflect that earlier in this paper I counseled against people too readily leaving the normal path of life and that I am now counseling a policy which is certain to create disturbance in individual lives, families and communities. That is so. But to depart from the common way in response or reaction to a conscription law, in the attempt to adapt oneself to an abnormal state of society, is one thing. To leave father, mother, wife, child, yea and one's own life also, at the behest of Christ or conscience is quite another. Our generation will not return to a condition under which every man may sit under his own vine and fig tree, with none to make him afraid, unless there are those who are willing to pay the high cost of redemption and deliverance from a regime of regimentation, terror and war.

Finally, it is of crucial importance that we should understand that for the individual to pit himself in Holy Disobedience against the war-making and conscripting State, wherever it or he be located, is not an act of despair or defeatism. Rather, I think we may say that precisely this individual refusal to "go along" is now the beginning and the core of any realistic and practical movement against war and for a more peaceful and brotherly world. For it becomes daily clearer that political and military leaders pay virtually no attention to protests against current foreign policy and pleas for peace when they know perfectly well that when it comes to a showdown, all but a handful of the millions of protesters will "go along" with the war to which the policy leads. All but a handful will submit to conscription. Few of the protesters will so much as risk their jobs in the cause of "peace." The failure of the policy-makers to change their course does not, save perhaps in very rare instances, mean that they are evil men who want war. They feel, as indeed they so often declare in crucial moments, that the issues are so complicated, the forces arrayed against them so strong, that they "have no choice" but to add another score of billions to the military budget, and so on and on. Why should they think there is any reality, hope or salvation in "peace advocates" who when the moment of decision comes also act on the assumption that they "have no choice" but to conform?

Precisely in a day when the individual appears to be utterly helpless, to "have no choice," when the aim of the "system" is to convince him that he is helpless as an individual and that the only way to meet regimentation is by regimentation, there is absolutely no hope save in going back to the beginning. The human being, the child of God, must assert his humanity and his sonship again. He must exercise the choice which he no longer has as something accorded him by society, which he "naked, weaponless, armourless, without shield or spear, but only with naked hands and open eyes" must create again. He must understand that this naked human being is the one *real* thing in the face of the mechanics and the mechanized institutions of our age. He, by the grace of God, is the seed of all the human life there will be on earth in the future, though he may have to die to make that harvest possible. As *Life* magazine stated in its unexpectedly profound and stirring editorial of August 20, 1945, its first issue after the atom bombing of Hiroshima: "Our sole safeguard against the very real danger of a reversion to barbarism is the kind of morality which compels the individual conscience, be the group right or wrong. The individual conscience against the atomic bomb? Yes. There is no other way."